Fluent in Spanish

The Best Tips & Tricks to Learn Spanish Super Fast

Maria Fernandez

Published by Maria Fernandez

Copyright © 2017 Maria Fernandez

Copyright © 2023 of this edition: Maria Fernandez

Copyright © Cover design: Maria Fernandez

ISBN: 978-0-9545320-9-3

All rights reserved. The content of this book may not be copied, distributed, loaned, extracted, published, recorded, displayed, modified or transferred in any form or by any means except with prior permission.

This title is available as audiobook, printed book and ebook.

To my friend Pedro, for the inspiration.

Contents

Spanish courses by Maria Fernandez	VII
Introduction	IX
About Maria Fernandez, your Spanish teacher	X
1. What you'll discover when you start learning Spanish	1
2. Why studying with a Spanish course is essential	3
3. How to love your Spanish course	8
4. How to go through the lessons in your Spanish course	10
5. How to develop your Spanish speaking skills	14
6. How to understand Spanish without trouble	16
7. How to learn Spanish words & remember them	18
8. How much Spanish grammar do you need?	21
9. How to get a great Spanish accent	24
10. How to communicate in Spanish after just a few lessons	26
11. How to keep up your motivation to learn Spanish	29
12. How to build the Spanish learning habit	32
13. How to enjoy learning Spanish	34
14. How to make the most of your Spanish learning time	37
15. 3 exercises to make super fast progress with Spanish	40
16. The 7 ugly Spanish learning myths	43

17. What to do when you finish your Spanish course	46
How to get the audiobook and printed book	48
Maria Fernandez's Spanish courses: details & links	49
How to contact Maria Fernandez	51
Please, review this book. ¡Gracias!	52

Spanish courses by Maria Fernandez

LL THESE COURSES ARE available at kerapido.com

You can find more details about each course at the end of this book.

- Learn Spanish at Your Own Pace - Printed book, ebook & audiobook

- Learn Spanish at Your Own Pace - Online course

- Spanish Verb Course - Step-by-step online course

- Spanish Verb Series – Books & audiobooks

- Spanish Audio Lessons for Complete Beginners - Audiobook & ebook

- Spanish Online Lessons

- Fluent in Spanish - Printed book, ebook & audiobook

- Sherlock Holmes Bilingual Story - Printed book, ebook & audiobook

- Sherlock Holmes Bilingual Story - Online course

- Spanish Course for Kids - Online course

- Spanish Video Lessons on YouTube

- Speak Spanish with Maria Fernandez – Podcast

To contact Maria Fernandez, go to **kerapido.com/contact**

To see Maria Fernandez's lessons & courses, go to **kerapido.com**

Introduction

How to become fluent in Spanish super fast

MY MISSION IS TO help you speak and understand Spanish. Not someday, but as fast as possible, without the pain and the overwhelm.

I want you to enjoy your Spanish lessons and look forward to them. That's why I've put together this little guide.

In it, I'm going to show you how to go through a Spanish lesson, step by step. We're going to see how you can develop your speaking and listening skills super fast. I'm going to give you the secret of how to learn words and remember them, how to develop a great Spanish accent, and how to stay motivated.

But let me start by introducing myself.

> "Thanks to words, we have been able to rise above the brutes; and thanks to words, we have often sunk to the level of the demons." – Aldous Huxley

About Maria Fernandez, your Spanish teacher

TEACHING AND LEARNING LANGUAGES is my passion, career and favourite pastime. I believe you can learn a foreign language at any age, if you set your mind to it. That's what my students have proved to me in my over twenty years of teaching.

It's a great privilege to help people become fluent in my mother tongue. Thanks to my students I find teaching Spanish exciting, fun and hugely rewarding.

My passion for languages goes back to my teenage years. Before I started teaching others, I taught myself several languages, including English. At first, I learned super slowly. Eventually, I developed a learning method which I've been perfecting ever since. Teaching myself has given me first hand experience of the difficulties every learner has, the ups and downs, and the frustrations.

Drawing from my teaching and learning experience, I'm now the author of several popular Spanish courses. You can find them all on **kerapido.com**

To find out more about me, go to **kerapido.com/about**

"If language had been the creation not of poetry but of logic, we should only have one." – Friedrich Hebbel

Chapter 1

What you'll discover when you start learning Spanish

Being able to speak a foreign language is one of the most rewarding achievements in life. But it requires patience and practice. Along the way, you're bound to find obstacles. Throughout this guide, I'll show you how to overcome them. Here are the 9 main obstacles you'll find:

Obstacle #1: you'll forget most of the words you come across in your lessons, at least once, even if you have an excellent memory. That's why revising your lessons is essential.

Obstacle #2: you'll find some days more difficult than others. Some grammar lessons will be impenetrable, some pronunciation rules confusing, and some basic numbers impossible to understand. Patience and perseverance will make things a lot easier.

Obstacle #3: the Spanish verbs can be overwhelming. For a while, you'll mix them up, and you'll forget their endings. Carry on, and you'll master them the way natives do.

Obstacle #4: every so often, you'll be tempted to give up. Follow my tips on how to boost your motivation, and you're guaranteed to become fluent.

Obstacle #5: now and them you'll come across words that you'll find difficult to pronounce, even if you know the rules well. With practice, you'll be able to say all Spanish words with a great accent.

Obstacle #6: some phrases and sentences will make little sense, even if you know their translation. To really understand them, you need to develop a "feeling" for the language. That'll come with practice.

Obstacle #7: the conversations in your lessons will sound fast, very fast. And not just the first time you listen to them. That's how Spanish people talk. Play the recordings in your course as often as you can, and you'll soon get used to the speed.

Obstacle #8: you can have big ups and downs. Some days, you'll feel you've forgotten half of what you've learned. Other days, your course conversations will sound easy, and you'll have little difficulty with the drills. Be kind to yourself. Whenever you have a bad day, focus on tasks you find easier and leave the more difficult ones for the next day.

Obstacle #9: often you'll find your motivation's gone, for no particular reason. That's why creating the habit of learning some Spanish every day is so important. In this guide, I'll show you how to do just that.

"A different language is a different vision of life." – Federico Fellini

Chapter 2

Why studying with a Spanish course is essential

No Spanish course is perfect, but without a course you'll never become fluent in Spanish.

There's a wide variety of good and affordable Spanish courses that you can buy or subscribe to. They teach you in different ways, emphasising different aspects of the language, and with a choice of formats and platforms.

The best way to choose the right course for you is to first answer these 6 questions:

- Do you want to learn Castilian Spanish or Latin American Spanish?
- What's your budget?
- Which level are you starting from?
- What are your main objectives: speaking, understanding, reading, and/or writing?

- Which format or formats do you prefer: book, audiobook, online course, video, app?

- Are you planning to learn on your own or will you have a teacher?

How to choose the best course for you

All good Spanish courses have these 8 features:

Feature #1: everyday conversations recorded by native Spanish speakers. Without recordings, you won't be able to develop your listening skills. You also won't be able to practise speaking, and you'll develop a poor accent.

Feature #2: the Spanish transcript and English translation of all the course conversations. This will save you precious time, and you won't have to use a dictionary.

Feature #3: vocabulary flashcards, preferably audio flashcards. That is, flashcards where you can read and hear the Spanish words, and see their English translation on the back. Vocabulary audio flashcards are the fastest, easiest and most fun way to learn words.

Feature #4: all nouns in the vocabulary flashcards should come with their article ("el problema", "la carne"), rather than on their own ("problema", "carne"). This will prevent you from making basic gender mistakes.

Feature #5: grammar lessons that blend with the rest of the material. Bad Spanish courses bring up grammar topics randomly, leaving you lost and frustrated. Good courses introduce you to the main topics gradually and in order.

Feature #6: speaking drills where you can practise putting words together in Spanish, step by step.

Feature #7: listening drills, so you can quickly understand Spanish without trouble.

Feature #8: pronunciation lessons and drills to develop a great accent.

Before buying them, all good Spanish courses give you a detailed description of their features, and offer you free samples. They also come with a full money-back guarantee. Courses without free samples or a full money-back guarantee are a risky choice.

The biggest advantage of getting a good Spanish course is that it allows you to focus on learning the language, rather than having to create your own course as you go along.

Having to create your own Spanish course is a sure path to failure, because it's very difficult and time-consuming. Let a good course guide you all the way, and you'll learn Spanish super fast.

When choosing a Spanish course, if you're unsure about your level, get a course for beginners. You should definitely do that if you've studied Spanish in the past, but haven't used it recently. In general, always get a course that's slightly below your current level. Far from being a waste of time, studying at a lower level helps you build a solid base with no gaps. And that allows you to learn Spanish a lot faster.

Important note: once you've chosen a Spanish course, stick to it, and go through it from beginning to end. Trust your course, and you're guaranteed to become fluent super fast.

Are you looking for a good Spanish course? Go to **kerapido.com/online**

Why choosing a free Spanish course is a bad idea

Over the years, I've reviewed dozens of free Spanish courses. Sadly, I've never come across one I could happily recommend to my students. Free courses cost you a lot of time and unnecessary pain. The 5 reasons for this are:

- Free courses are often created by amateurs with little knowledge of how to teach Spanish.

- Free courses are plagued with errors, often basic and serious errors: gender, verb conjugation, translation of basic words, pronunciation rules, spelling, etc. Some of the errors I've seen are the equivalent of saying in English: "He eat oringes" or 'We goes to Europa".

- The recordings in free courses, when they have them, are usually made by non-native speakers. That'll give you bad pronunciation habits, which you'll find difficult to get rid of.

- Free courses are incomplete. They cover little vocabulary, and have frustrating gaps.

- Free courses throw the material at you randomly, so you have to figure out for yourself what to learn next. That's not an easy task when you're a beginner.

Studying with a Spanish teacher

Nothing will help you learn faster than an experienced native Spanish teacher that encourages you to speak. It's a more expensive option than learning on your own, but the boost to your motivation will be huge.

If you want to learn Spanish with me, I offer some very affordable lessons. You can join my live online classes, and practise speaking and listening.

To join my live lessons, go to: **kerapido.com/class**

My thoughts on total immersion

Landing in a foreign country with little or no knowledge of the language, and with the intention of learning it "the way children do", is likely to be a disastrous waste of your time and money.

The main reason for it is that what you get from total immersion mostly depends on how much you know when you embark on it. Basically, when you immerse yourself in a foreign language, the higher your level is when you start the more you'll learn. If you're a beginner, the experience will be frustrating. You'll soon find yourself surrounded by non-Spanish speakers and avoiding people who cannot communicate with you in English.

Also, learning the Spanish verbs just from talking to native speakers will take you years. With a good verb course you can master the verbs in only a few months.

To make the most of total immersion, learn as much Spanish as you can before travelling abroad.

"Language is the dress of thought." – Samuel Johnson

Chapter 3

How to love your Spanish course

Once you've chosen the course you're going to study with, it's a good idea to familiarise yourself with it before you start Lesson 1. Familiarising yourself with your course will help you:

- See how it's structured.
- Find out which topics are covered.
- Get a feeling for how long the lessons are.
- See how many exercises and drills each lesson has.
- Get an idea of how much vocabulary you'll be learning.
- Know how much grammar you're expected to learn.
- See what you can do in just five or ten minutes here and there.
- Get a rough idea of how long it'll take you to finish the course.

The better you know what your Spanish course brings you, the less overwhelming it'll be.

How to familiarise yourself with your Spanish course

It'll only take you ten or fifteen minutes to see what your new Spanish course looks like. Whether it's a book, online course, audio course, app or set of video lessons, your course will have a table of contents. Go to that table of contents and look at how many lessons there are. Then look at how many pages, videos or mp3s each lesson has. On the table of contents, read the headings for each lesson to find out which topics are covered.

Next, flip through the pages in your course, or navigate through it, to get a feeling for what the course looks like, how long each section is, how many questions the drills have, how many sections are recorded, etc. By now, your Spanish course will look a lot more attractive and less threatening.

Once you start your course, browsing through the lessons to come should also be part of your routine. After you finish a lesson, have a quick glance at the next one before you plunge into it. This will help you look forward to learning and avoid procrastination.

> "The limits of my language mean the limits of my world." – Ludwig Wittgenstein

Chapter 4

How to go through the lessons in your Spanish course

THE SIMPLEST WAY TO teach yourself Spanish is to follow the tips in this guide. How you go through your Spanish course is going to determine how fast you learn the language. Here are 4 very useful tips:

Tip #1: don't skip anything.

Whether you're a complete beginner or have some previous knowledge of Spanish, start your course on lesson 1. Don't skip any lessons or sections, even if you're familiar with them.

I cannot emphasise enough the importance of building a solid base. The more solid your knowledge of basic Spanish is, the faster you'll learn new things.

Tip #2: don't rush.

Avoid rushing through the first few lessons of your course, even if they're easy. Go through them thoroughly, repeating the drills until you can get all the answers right. That way you'll avoid gaps in your knowledge. Small gaps at the beginning become huge holes by lesson twelve.

Tip #3: trust your course.

Sometimes you may feel that your course goes too fast, or not fast enough. Often you'll get the impression that a difficult grammar point is brought up too soon, or that essential vocabulary isn't coming up soon enough.

Put those thoughts aside and follow the material in the way it's presented. Avoid jumping to more advanced lessons or using two language courses at the same time. It'll all soon fall into place!

Tip #4: take notes if you need to.

Don't hesitate to write notes down in your notebook, or create a document on your computer called, for example: "My Spanish course notes". Make a note of anything you find difficult or unclear, and come back to your notes every so often. As you progress, you'll see that it all becomes clear and the difficulties disappear.

Let's go through a Spanish lesson, step by step

For this, I'm going to use my Spanish online course at **kerapido.com/online** as an example.

The first thing to do when you start a new lesson, including Lesson 1, is to listen to the recorded conversation twice, without looking at its transcript or translation. Always make sure you listen to your conversations before reading their transcript. Often you'll understand very little or even nothing at first, but it's the most effective way to develop your listening skills fast.

Then listen to the conversation again, this time while you read the Spanish transcript. After that, go through the English translation.

Now listen to the conversation again, and read it out loud along with the recording. Make sure you speak out loud, as if you were talking to someone. Speaking a foreign language often requires you to produce sounds you're not used to. You'll make many mistakes at first. You'll get stuck and won't be able to string words together the way you do in your native language. By reading sentences out loud, you'll overcome those difficulties, and you'll get a great accent.

Then go through the conversation line by line. This is an excellent way of developing your speaking skills.

Once you're familiar with the conversation, move on to the vocabulary. If your course has audio flashcards, play them several times. Say the Spanish words out loud, making sure you understand every word on the flashcards. Once you're familiar with the vocabulary, play the conversation once more. Notice how you can understand it more easily now.

Then move on to the pronunciation rules and practice. Read out the words in that section, focusing on the sounds you're learning. If your course has pronunciation audio flashcards, play them until you can say all the words without hesitation.

Then move on to the grammar section. Make sure you don't skip any points. Then do all the speaking, listening and other drills in your lesson. Don't skip any. Redo the drills until you can get all the answers right.

Before you move on to a new lesson, always revise the one you've just done.

In my Spanish online course I take you through the 24 lessons, following these steps in each of them. That way you never have to wonder what to do next, and you can focus on learning super fast.

The magic of revising

Revising is essential if you want to learn Spanish fast. Without revision, you'll forget most of what you've learned, even if you have a good memory. Revising will boost your motivation to continue learning, and it'll close any gaps you may have in your knowledge.

Go back to the lessons you've completed in your course as often as you can. I always advice my students to revise at least 50% of the time they're studying. The more you play your course conversations, vocabulary flashcards, and drills, the faster you'll learn.

Completing your Spanish course

Once you finish the last lesson in your Spanish course, don't move on to a new course. Not immediately. Instead, go through all the lessons one more time.

Make sure you can understand all the conversations without looking at their transcript. Play all the vocabulary flashcards. Redo the drills fast, until you can easily get all the answers right. Play the speaking drills and aim at saying whole sentences at the same speed as the recordings.

Remember: going through your course a second time will put you a lot closer to becoming fluent in Spanish.

> "One does not inhabit a country; one inhabits a language. That is our country, our fatherland - and no other." – E. M. Cioran

Chapter 5

How to develop your Spanish speaking skills

THE EASIEST WAY TO develop your speaking skills fast is to speak Spanish from day one, and to continue practising every day. The easiest way to get yourself to speak every day is with a good Spanish course.

A good course will take you step by step, and will help you build your confidence, one sentence at a time. There are 2 easy exercises that will skyrocket your speaking skills. They are:

Exercise #1: line by line conversations.

Being able to play the conversations in your Spanish course line by line will do wonders for you. Play a line and say it out loud, along with the recording. At first, you'll be unable to keep up with it, but with practice you'll get better every day.

To make fast progress, the secret is to focus on one line at a time. Instead of racing through all the lines in a conversation, focus on each and every line. Say it out loud several times until you're comfortable with it. This is one of the exercises I often did to become fluent in English.

Are you looking for a Spanish course with everyday conversations that you can play line by line? Have a look at my Spanish online course at **kerapido.com/online**

Exercise #2: speaking flashcards.

Speaking flashcards give you an English sentence on one side, and you're asked to say it out loud in Spanish. When you flip the flashcard, you can see the sentence in Spanish, and you can play it to hear it. As you get on with your Spanish course, the sentences you get on your flashcards become more complex.

Speaking flashcards are a great way to develop your conversation skills. Speaking Spanish can be scary. By doing exercises that take you step by step, you're much more likely to become fluent fast.

In my Spanish online course there are plenty of exercises with speaking flashcards to help you step by step.

> "There are seven days in a week and 'someday' isn't one of them." – Anonymous.

Chapter 6

How to understand Spanish without trouble

THE BEST WAY TO develop your listening skills is to listen to lots of Spanish. But not just any Spanish.

When you listen to radio shows, music, films and TV programmes you make painfully slow progress. To make super fast progress, the secret is to focus on the conversations in your Spanish course.

Listen to those conversations regularly and often. Become familiar with all the words. Master the common expressions. That way you'll build a sound knowledge of basic Spanish that will allow you understand the language without trouble. To skyrocket your listening skills, there's one magic exercise.

The magic exercise: listening before reading

Whenever you come across a new conversation in your Spanish course, play it before reading its Spanish transcript or English translation.

You'll understand next to nothing the first time you play it. That's OK. Play it again and try to catch a word or two. Then, read the transcript. Play the same conversation a few more times. Notice how you start to understand a few more words. For a while, you'll find this a frustrating exercise. But the results are amazing and well worth the discomfort.

In my Spanish online course, I walk you step by step through the conversations, so you can develop your listening skills super fast. To see how this works, go to **kerapido.com/online**

"To have another language is to possess a second soul." – Charlemagne

Chapter 7

How to learn Spanish words & remember them

Forgetting Spanish words is frustrating. It kills your motivation to continue learning the language. That's why you need to make sure you can learn words fast, and remember them. Here are my 4 best tips for learning Spanish words fast:

Tip #1: use vocabulary audio flashcards.

The easiest and fastest way to learn Spanish words is with audio flashcards. But those flashcards cannot be random words from random lists. Instead, they have to be words that have come up in the conversations you've listened to in your course.

By hearing Spanish words both in your conversations and audio flashcards, you'll become familiar with those words super fast, and you'll remember them forever.

To revise the vocabulary in your course, play the audio flashcards as often as you can. Say the words out loud, along with the recordings; and check that you're familiar with their translation.

Tip #2: learn all nouns with "el" and "la".

Make sure you learn all Spanish nouns with their article ("el" or "la") rather than on their own. Whenever you learn a Spanish noun with its article, you're avoiding future mistakes. You're also saving yourself a lot of time and unnecessary work, because you won't have to go back to relearn it.

The Spanish gender rules can help you "guess" the gender of many nouns, especially those ending in "a" and "o", but there are many nouns that will let you down if you try to guess their gender. That's why it's safer and faster to learn all nouns with their article when you first come across them.

To help you learn fast, the vocabulary audio flashcards in my Spanish online course give you all nouns with their article.

Tip #3: learn phrases as a whole.

Avoid analysing phrases word for word. Instead, learn phrases as a whole, for example: "de vez en cuando" (from time to time), "de nada" (you're welcome). When possible, learn phrases in context, as part of complete sentences. That way you'll remember them more easily.

Tip #4: find similarities between words.

If you can find a similarity between a Spanish word you've just come across (for example: "las verduras" - the vegetables) and another Spanish word you already know (for example: "verde" - green), you won't forget it easily.

In my Spanish online course there's a "Words with Similarities" section in each lesson to help you remember words super fast.

> "... words, like Nature, half reveal
> And half conceal the Soul within." –
> Alfred Tennyson

Chapter 8

How much Spanish grammar do you need?

LEARNING SOME GRAMMAR WILL allow you to become fluent in Spanish. Without a knowledge of grammar, you'll never get there. Knowing some grammar is essential for using the right verb form and tense, the right ending with describing words, and the right word order, among other things.

Learning grammar doesn't have to be dull. A good Spanish course will introduce you to the main grammar topics in an easy and practical way. It'll also give you exercises and drills to practise them. By the end of your Spanish course you should be familiar with:

- How to build the regular verb forms.
- How to conjugate the main irregular verbs.
- The gender rules.
- How articles, nouns and adjectives go together.

- How to build questions and statements.
- Basic word order.

Your course might also cover, in more or less detail: prepositions, negative words, possessives, pronouns, adverbs, etc.

Once you've done some Spanish, you may find yourself wanting to learn more grammar than your course offers you. If that's the case, avoid starting a grammar course before finishing your current Spanish course. First, go through all the lessons in your course. Then, get a grammar course and focus on it. You'll get a lot more out of it that way.

How to learn Spanish grammar

If you find that the whole concept of grammar is too alien to you, it's a good idea to get an English grammar guide first and familiarise yourself with the main topics. Preferably, do that before you start learning Spanish. In a few days you'll be up to scratch.

For recommendations on good English grammar books, go to: **kerapido.com/english**

Here are my 3 tips on how to learn Spanish grammar fast:

Tip #1: grammar lessons are there to help you.

Always read the grammar lessons in your Spanish course carefully. Don't skip any of them, and don't rush through the topics you find easy. You may miss something crucial.

Tip #2: grammar drills are your best friend.

Complete all the grammar exercises and drills in your lessons, however easy or difficult they are. Repeat them until you can get all the answers right.

Tip #3: finding similarities is magic.

When you're learning grammar, look for similarities with topics you're already familiar with. For example, try to find similarities between regular and irregular verb endings, the word order in questions and statements, noun and adjective endings, etc.

Once you finish your Spanish course, it's likely that you'll want to learn the Spanish verbs in more depth. To see the Spanish verb courses I recommend, go to: **kerapido.com/grammar**

> "Language most shows a man; speak that I may see thee." – Ben Jonson

Chapter 9

How to get a great Spanish accent

The only secret to a great Spanish accent is regular practice with good exercises. Focusing on your Spanish pronunciation may not be an obvious thing to do as a beginner, but it has 4 superb advantages:

Advantage #1: the better your accent is, the better native speakers will understand you.

Advantage #2: the better your accent is, the better you'll understand native speakers.

Advantage #3: having a good accent from the start allows you to avoid bad pronunciation habits that are difficult to get rid of later on.

Advantage #4: having a good accent is hugely rewarding and motivating.

Getting a good accent requires patience and practice. There's no way around it. But once you start working on your pronunciation you'll notice an improvement immediately. Guaranteed!

How to work on your Spanish accent

When I was learning English, I spent a lot of time working on my accent. Looking back, both personally and professionally, the results have by far outweighed the effort.

That's why all the Spanish courses I've created over the years include pronunciation lessons, listening drills, speaking exercises, and accent tips. A course without good pronunciation lessons isn't worth your time, because it won't help you develop the accent you deserve. Here are my 6 tips on how to get a great Spanish accent:

Tip #1: make sure you learn only from native Spanish speakers.

Tip #2: focus on your Spanish accent from lesson 1. You'll make many basic mistakes for a while, but you'll soon notice your improvement.

Tip #3: remember that the more Spanish you hear, and the more speaking practice you have, the better your pronunciation will be. Reading out the conversations in your course, practising the vocabulary out loud, and saying the drills out loud, will all improve your accent.

Tip #4: go through the pronunciation rules in your Spanish course carefully. Compare the way letters are pronounced in English and Spanish.

Tip #5: go back to the pronunciation rules in your course as often as necessary.

Tip #6: read out all the words in your pronunciation flashcards. Saying them quietly or in your head will be of little help. To develop a good accent you need to say them out loud, as if you were talking to someone.

"Words, once printed, have a life of their own." – Carol Burnett

Chapter 10

How to communicate in Spanish after just a few lessons

Being able to communicate well in Spanish as a beginner is a great motivation to continue learning the language.

Mastering Spanish will take you time, but you can start using your first sentences within a few lessons. You'll be able to have simple Spanish conversations even if you only know a couple of hundred words, some expressions, and a few verb forms.

To communicate well in Spanish when you only know the basics, here are my 6 tips:

Tip #1: speak loud and clear.

When we lose our confidence, we tend to lower the volume. Often the reason why people don't get what we're saying is because they cannot hear it, not because they cannot understand us.

Tip #2: keep your sentences short.

Long sentences are much more difficult to master. It's easy to get their word order wrong, making them meaningless. For a while you may only be able to say simple sentences, but if you can say them clearly and with confidence you'll be able to get by in most situations.

Tip #3: use words you can pronounce well.

If a word you cannot say clearly is essential, practice saying it until others can understand it. If all the Spanish words you know can be understood by Spanish speakers when you say them, those words will take you a long way.

Tip #4: think ahead what it is you're going to say.

If you're going shopping, check the words for the items you're looking for. If you're going to a restaurant, check your food and drink vocabulary.

Tip #5: think of the possible answers you may get.

Check the vocabulary that's likely to come up when people talk to you, and familiarise yourself with it.

Tip #6: master the numbers.

Numbers come up in almost every conversation, and native speakers always say them fast. Get into the habit of practising the Spanish numbers regularly.

Remember: people like being addressed to in their language, especially in their own country. Making the effort to communicate in Spanish will earn you lots of new friends!

"If you talk to a man in a language he understands, that goes to his head. If you talk to him in his own language, that goes to his heart." – Nelson Mandela

Chapter 11

How to keep up your motivation to learn Spanish

MOTIVATION WILL MAKE YOU fluent in Spanish super fast.

Taking up a foreign language is easy for many of us. The difficulty is in finding the motivation to persevere, and the power to ignore the negative thoughts that lead to failure. Fortunately, motivation doesn't just come naturally or not at all. There's a lot you can do to boost it. Here are my 9 tips:

Tip #1: learn some Spanish every day.

Even if it's just a few words. With a mobile-friendly course, it's easy to listen to a conversation, play some audio flashcards, or do a drill, wherever you are. Knowing that you've got a bit closer to your goal is a great booster. Remember: you don't need to speak fluently to get by, so every word you learn really counts.

Tip #2: think of all the benefits of learning Spanish.

It'll make you more independent when travelling abroad, it'll save you money when you shop away from stores catering for tourists, and it'll help you make new friends. It can even help you in your career and family life.

Tip #3: be kind to yourself.

Aim for short-term goals, like finishing one lesson per week. If you try hard but cannot achieve your goal, set yourself a more realistic one for the following week.

Tip #4: ignore naysayers and cynics.

They're everywhere. Their negative comments can be a big blow to your motivation, especially if they come at the wrong time. Ignore those gratuitous comments or, even better, take them as a challenge.

Tip #5: embrace the language difficulties.

Don't let them overwhelm you. Patience is a great ally. Things that don't make sense today will be clear in a couple of weeks. The more you learn, the more everything will fit into place.

Tip #6: remember that motivation's worst enemy is boredom.

To keep it at bay, have short learning sessions of no more than twenty minutes each. If you have time, take a short break and then continue with a second session. Always stop before getting bored. That way you'll look forward to tomorrow's session.

Tip #7: slow progress is a huge demotivator.

To learn Spanish super fast, spot those "lost minutes" in your day when you could be learning some Spanish. Play your lessons while you wait in a queue or sit on a train. Make a habit of having your Spanish course at hand. You can learn hundreds of words in those "lost minutes".

Tip #8: look back and celebrate.

Every so often, as you get on with your Spanish course, browse the material you've covered to see how much progress you've made. Have you noticed how many words you learned last week? How much more grammar you know now? How many things that seemed difficult only a month ago are now easy? Finishing your Spanish course is just a few lessons away.

Tip #9: reward yourself.

That's a trick that never fails to boost motivation. The greatest reward I can think of is a visit to a Spanish-speaking country. On the weeks leading to your trip, you'll learn faster than ever before. If travelling abroad isn't something you can do, I encourage you to join my live Spanish online classes. I'd love to see you there. To find out more, go to **kerapido.com/class**

Every day that you persevere with your Spanish makes you more positive and motivated. It gives you that indescribable sense of achievement that comes with learning a foreign language.

When your motivation gets down, remember that the only thing preventing you from reaching your goal are your negative thoughts. Think positive and you'll become fluent in Spanish super fast.

> "Language is the inventory of human experience." – L. W. Lockhart

Chapter 12

How to build the Spanish learning habit

HABITS PUT LEARNING ON steroids. They kill procrastination, remove excuses, and leave a clean path for fast and steady progress. To build your Spanish learning habit, follow these 6 easy steps:

Step #1: start small.

Even better, start very small. On day 1, do only two minutes of Spanish. Play a conversation in your Spanish course or a few vocabulary flashcards. No more. On day 2, do three minutes. On day 3, do four minutes. Soon you'll be doing ten or twenty minutes without feeling overwhelmed.

Step #2: make it convenient.

Use a Spanish course that suits your lifestyle. Forcing yourself to sit down and free up an hour won't work. You'll find yourself procrastinating. Instead, go for a course that blends into your daily routine. Online courses and courses you can download to your phone and tablet are ideal.

Step #3: make it daily.

It's better to learn for ten minutes every day than two hours once a week. You'll make faster progress, and you'll look forward to playing your Spanish course, instead of dreading it.

Step #4: make it predictable.

Find a daily time slot and stick to it. For example, play your Spanish course on your commute or during your lunch break. That'll help you avoid procrastination, and will get rid of the stress of having to find the time every day.

Step #5: have micro goals.

Most goals we think of in life are too vague, for example: "I want to become fluent in Spanish one day". They're not only vague, they're also scary. That's why we rarely achieve them.

Instead, think tiny. Have achievable weekly and daily goals. For example, "I'm going to finish one lesson per week" or "I'm going to do three drills every day". Achieving your daily micro goals will make you fluent in Spanish, and you'll enjoy learning.

Step #6: allow for imperfection.

When you let yourself down and miss a goal, avoid dwelling on the negative. Instead, think of what you can do to stay on target. Is there a better time slot for your Spanish lessons? Would a different type of course be more convenient?

Remember: the secret is to make it impossible for you to say "NO" to your Spanish lessons. Do that, and you'll become fluent super fast.

> "You can't see other people's point of view when you have only one language." – Frank Smith

Chapter 13

How to enjoy learning Spanish

THE MORE YOU ENJOY learning Spanish, the more Spanish you'll learn; and the faster you'll learn it. Here are 10 ideas on how to look forward to your Spanish lessons:

Idea #1: make it a no-brainer.

Use a course that fits into your lifestyle. The more convenient your course is for you, the more you'll use it.

Idea #2: make it a tiny effort.

Focusing on your Spanish lessons for just ten or twenty minutes at a time is doable, and it brings great results.

Idea #3: don't make it a lonely experience.

Learn Spanish with your partner, friends, colleagues, children or neighbours. It'll be much more fun.

Idea #4: change the scenery.

With modern technology you can learn Spanish wherever you are: car, train, bus or plane; out walking, while waiting, during lunch, and even in the bath.

Idea #5: get social.

Find Spanish speaking people on your favourite social media sites.

Idea #6: make friends.

Get to know some Spanish speakers in your community.

Idea #7: find a guide.

Get a teacher or join an online class. They're fun and you'll learn a lot faster.

Idea #8: love the challenge.

Spanish will get tricky at times. When it does, take a step back and redo some of your course drills, listen to the conversations again, or practise reading out some sentences. Everything will soon get easier.

Idea #9: set yourself realistic goals.

The secret is to go for doable daily goals. Achieving your goals, no matter how small they are, will not only help you enjoy learning, it'll also save you from procrastination. Taking it one day at a time is how you'll become fluent in Spanish fast.

Idea #10: stay positive.

It's easy to get drowned by the thought of how much you still have to learn. But remember that every word you learn counts.

"Language is the road map of a culture. It tells you where its people come from and where they are going." – Rita Mae Brown

Chapter 14

How to make the most of your Spanish learning time

If you make good use of your Spanish learning time your progress will be amazing. But how do you make good use of your time?

There are superb ways of learning, and then there are dreadful ways of wasting your time and getting nowhere. Here are the 4 superb ways:

Superb way #1: study at the right level.

If you're not sure about your level in Spanish, get a course that covers some material you already know. The idea here is to never study above your level. Otherwise you'd be wasting time looking up words you're supposed to know, and you'd develop gaps in your knowledge.

Superb way #2: focus on your lessons.

Remove all distractions (social media, TV, phone ...), and you'll learn in twenty minutes what can otherwise take several hours.

Superb way #3: go through your lessons several times.

Study each lesson in your Spanish course not just once, but several times. As we saw, revising is an essential part of language learning. If you only go through your lessons once, you'll soon forget most of what you've learned. And you'll also develop gaps that will prevent you from making progress.

Superb way #4: listen carefully and often.

Play the recordings in your Spanish course as often as you can. The more you listen to the conversations the faster you'll develop your listening skills. The more you listen to the audio flashcards, the faster you'll expand your vocabulary.

Those are the superb ways of learning Spanish. There are also dreadful ways of wasting your time, which you must avoid. The main 3 are:

Dreadful way #1: making lists of words.

Self-proclaimed language gurus love recommending that you spend endless hours creating word lists. The problem is, word lists are a sure path to failure. They're boring, slow, and a total waste of your precious time and energy. You'll never remember more than a handful of words from a list after a couple of days.

Instead, focus on the vocabulary audio flashcards in your Spanish course. They're the best tool for learning new words.

Dreadful way #2: using more than one course at a time.

Jumping from one Spanish course to another, from one website to another, will drain your energy. You'll spend half of your time wondering what to study next.

Instead, use only one course; the one you like best and suits your lifestyle. That way all you need to do is resume where you stopped the day before.

Remember: the smaller the effort, the faster you'll learn.

Dreadful way #3: skipping the material you dislike.

Skipping material in your Spanish course will leave you with gaps. Don't skip any part of your lessons, however easy or irrelevant it may seem to you. Skipping material often leads to confusion.

Instead, go through all the sections in your course thoroughly. You won't regret it when you start making super fast progress!

> "The magic of the tongue is the most dangerous of all spells." – Edward Bulwer-Lytton

Chapter 15

3 exercises to make super fast progress with Spanish

WHEN I WAS STUDYING English I often did these three exercises. If you want to learn Spanish amazingly fast, they're the best. The ideal time to do these exercises is when you're revising, rather than the first time you go through a lesson. If you do them frequently, your progress will go up exponentially.

Exercise #1: reading out loud.

Whenever you go through the conversations in your Spanish course, don't stop at getting the gist of them. Instead, over a number of weeks, read them out loud, along with the recordings, until you can keep up with the speakers.

Doing this exercise frequently will skyrocket your speaking skills. Line by line conversations, like the ones in my Spanish online course, are the ideal way to do this exercise.

Exercise #2: dictation.

Do dictations from the conversations in your Spanish course. This is the best way to do this exercise: have pen and paper handy, or a device where you can type text in. Go to the first conversation in your course and play it through. Just listen to the conversation carefully, without typing or writing anything down. Make sure you don't look at the transcript.

Then play the conversation again, but this time pause it after a few words or a sentence. Write down what you've heard. Then play a few more words, pause the recording, and write down the new words. Write down the whole conversation this way. Then play it through one more time and check whether you need to amend anything.

Once you're done, compare what you've written with the conversation transcript. Make a note of the words you've got wrong. Keep your dictation for future reference. A week or two later, do the same dictation again. Compare the two and notice your improvement!

Exercise #3: translation.

Translate the conversations in your course back into Spanish. This exercise will be quite hard the first few times you try it. You'll make many mistakes, but it'll soon get easier. This is the ideal way to do this exercise:

Go to the English translation of the first conversation in your course. Make sure you cannot see the Spanish transcript. Write your translation down, one Spanish sentence at a time, or type it in. If you cannot remember a word or phrase, leave a gap.

When you're done, go to the Spanish transcript of that conversation and compare it with your translation. Mark the mistakes you've made, and keep your translation for future reference.

A couple of weeks later, redo the same translation. You'll find that many of your original mistakes have now vanished, and you can translate the whole conversation faster!

"In general, every country has the language it deserves." – Jorge Luis Borges

Chapter 16

The 7 ugly Spanish learning myths

MYTH #1: YOU'RE TOO old to learn Spanish.

I've been teaching Spanish for over twenty years. I've had many students in their sixties and seventies who've learned without trouble. Their enthusiasm is awe-inspiring. Their memories might not be what they were thirty years ago, but their patience, determination and common sense more than make up for it.

Remember: age isn't a barrier to language learning. A negative attitude is.

Myth #2: you cannot learn Spanish on your own.

This is just another ugly myth. Fortunately it's just that, a myth.

I, myself, have learned on my own most of the English, French, German, Italian, Portuguese and Japanese that I know today. Many of my students have come to me for private lessons after reaching an intermediate or even advanced level by themselves.

With a good course, you can become fluent in Spanish on your own, without question.

Myth #3: you can learn Spanish with that old course you found in the attic.

Only if you want to get very bored, waste a lot of time, and make little progress.

Technology has revolutionised language learning. Today you can get Spanish courses you could hardly dream of even five years ago. Spanish courses now have many more and better quality recordings. They often have interactive speaking and listening drills, pronunciation tools, videos, progress monitoring, audio flashcards, and a whole set of other features that render old courses totally obsolete.

Many of those new courses cost around $100 or less. If you want to learn Spanish super fast, they're a great investment.

Myth #4: you need to have a perfect Spanish accent to be understood.

No, you don't. Aim at clarity, rather than perfection, and everyone will understand you from the beginning. As long as your accent is clear and you avoid certain pronunciation mistakes, you'll have no trouble communicating in Spanish.

A good Spanish course will teach you which pronunciation mistakes to avoid. It'll show you the sounds you need to focus on, and it'll give you pronunciation drills. Developing a good Spanish accent is straightforward when you do your pronunciation drills.

Myth #5: you can skip the grammar, if you just want to learn to speak.

To be able to build even simple sentences, you need to know some grammar. If you skip the grammar, you'll soon get confused, and you'll never become fluent in Spanish.

Learning some grammar will allow you to make quick progress. You'll be able to understand people better, and you'll speak with more confidence. Mastering some Spanish grammar is well within your reach, and it's absolutely worth the effort!

Myth #6: learning languages is boring.

Slow progress is what makes language learning a bore. Forgetting what you've learned, not knowing what to study next, and needing a dictionary, all make Spanish learning a drag.

Bad courses are boring, but learning Spanish can easily be fun. Throughout this short book I've shown you how to stay motivated, develop your speaking skills, learn words super fast, and a lot more. Follow those tips and you'll enjoy learning Spanish. Guaranteed!

Myth #7: you can only learn Spanish in a Spanish-speaking country.

Learning abroad works best when you've completed at least one Spanish course. If you're at an intermediate or advanced level, learning in a Spanish-speaking country can be one of the most memorable experiences in your life. But if you're a beginner, it can be truly daunting, and almost certainly a waste of time and money.

Learn all the Spanish you can before traveling abroad, and you'll get a lot more out of it.

> "Language is the most human thing there is. It is a privilege of mankind... Each word carries within itself a life, a state, a feeling." – Carmen Conde

Chapter 17

What to do when you finish your Spanish course

WHEN YOU REACH THE end of your Spanish course, don't put it aside. Not for a while.

Before you move on to another course, you should revise all your lessons one more time. You'll get a lot more out of your course if you spend a bit longer on it. The best way to go about it is this:

- Go back to lesson 1. Listen to the conversations. Play the vocabulary flashcards. Do all the drills.

- Over the next few days, go through all your course lessons in order. Don't skip anything. Pay attention to the things you're still finding difficult, and spend a bit more time on them. Try playing the drills faster. Can you get all the answers right when you do?

Remember: a sound knowledge of basic Spanish will help you become fluent a lot faster.

To save you time, in my Spanish online course I walk you through your lesson revision. All you need to do is follow the steps as I present them to you. There's no guesswork. That way you can focus on becoming fluent super fast.

> "You can never understand one language until you understand at least two." – Geoffrey Willans & Ronald Searle

How to get the audiobook and printed book

T**O GET THE AUDIOBOOK** and printed book versions of Fluent in Spanish, this book, go to: **kerapido.com/fluent**

Maria Fernandez's Spanish courses: details & links

O VER THE YEARS I'VE created a number of Spanish courses and other material. You can find their free samples at **kerapido.com/free**

My courses and lessons come in different formats to help you learn Spanish fast wherever you are. Here are their titles and where to find them:

Learn Spanish at Your Own Pace – Online: interactive course with everyday conversations, vocabulary audio flashcards, pronunciation lessons, speaking and listening drills, quizzes, and more. Get the free samples and details at **kerapido.com/online**

Learn Spanish at Your Own Pace - Book & recordings: the book + audio version of the course above. Get the free samples and details at **kerapido.com/book**

Spanish Verb Course – Online: step-by-step videos with clear explanations, speaking practice, and listening drills. To see how this verb course works, go to **kerapido.com/verbs**

Spanish Verb Series – Books & audiobooks: single topic publications with step-by-step explanations, speaking practice, and listening drills. Find out more: **kerapido.com/verbs**

Spanish Audio Lessons for Complete Beginners – Audiobook & transcript: step-by-step lessons where I encourage you to speak with me from day 1. Get the free samples at **kerapido.com/audio**

Spanish Online Lessons – Live: join my live online group classes. There you can practise speaking and listening; and you can ask me your questions. For more details, go to **kerapido.com/class**

Fluent in Spanish – Book & audiobook: audio version of this book, read by me. Get the free sample and more details at **kerapido.com/fluent**

Sherlock Holmes Bilingual Story – Book: my Spanish translation of the Sherlock Holmes story "A Scandal in Bohemia" (Un escándalo en Bohemia). A parallel text edition with glossary. For more details, go to **kerapido.com/story**

Sherlock Holmes in Spanish – Audiobook: Spanish recording of "Un escándalo en Bohemia" (my translation of the Sherlock Holmes story "A Scandal in Bohemia"). Narrated by me, Maria Fernandez. To hear the free sample, go to **kerapido.com/story**

Spanish Video Lessons on YouTube: my short Spanish video lessons with speaking and listening drills. Watch them at **kerapido.com/youtube**

Speak Spanish with Maria Fernandez: my free podcast. Subscribe to it at **kerapido.com/podcast**

How to contact Maria Fernandez

D<small>O YOU HAVE ANY</small> questions, queries, suggestions, complaints or comments? To get in touch with me, go to: **kerapido.com/contact**

Please, review this book. ¡Gracias!

THANK YOU FOR READING this book. Let others know what you think about it. Write a short review on your online store.

Please be fair. Please be kind.

> "Uttering a word is like striking a note on the keyboard of the imagination." – Ludwig Wittgenstein

www.ingramcontent.com/pod-product-compliance
Lightning Source LLC
Chambersburg PA
CBHW051958290426
44110CB00015B/2289